OBOE

MOVIE FAVORITES

Solos and Band Arrangements
Correlated with Essential Elements Band Method

Arranged by
MICHAEL SWEENEY

T0052832

Welcome to Essential Elements Movie Favorites! There are two versions of each selection in this versatile book. The SOLO version appears on the left-hand page of your book. The FULL BAND arrangement appears on the right-hand page. Optional accompaniment recordings are available separately in CD or cassette format. Use these recordings when playing solos for friends and family.

ISBN 978-0-7935-5958-9

HAL•LEONARD® CORPORATION

7777 W. BLUEMOUND RD. P.O. BOX 13819 MILWAUKEE, WI 53213

00860014

From The Universal Motion Picture JURASSIC PARK

Theme From "JURASSIC PARK"

OBOE
Solo

Composed by JOHN WILLIAMS
Arranged by MICHAEL SWEENEY

MCA music publishing

From The Universal Motion Picture JURASSIC PARK

Theme From "JURASSIC PARK"

OBOE
Band Arrangement

Composed by JOHN WILLIAMS
Arranged by MICHAEL SWEENEY

0860014

MCA music publishing

From CHARIOTS OF FIRE
CHARIOTS OF FIRE

OBOE
Solo

Music by VANGELIS
Arranged by MICHAEL SWEENEY

00860014

CHARIOTS OF FIRE

OBOE
Band Arrangement

Music by VANGELIS
Arranged by MICHAEL SWEENEY

00860014

From THE MAN FROM SNOWY RIVER

THE MAN FROM SNOWY RIVER

(Main Title Theme)

OBOE
Solo

By BRUCE ROWLAND
Arranged by MICHAEL SWEENEY

From THE MAN FROM SNOWY RIVER

THE MAN FROM SNOWY RIVER
(Main Title Theme)

OBOE
Band Arrangement

By BRUCE ROWLAND
Arranged by MICHAEL SWEENEY

00860014

From The Paramount Motion Picture FORREST GUMP

FORREST GUMP - MAIN TITLE
(Feather Theme)

OBOE
Solo

Music by ALAN SILVESTRI
Arranged by MICHAEL SWEENEY

FORREST GUMP - MAIN TITLE
(Feather Theme)

OBOE
Band Arrangement

Music by ALAN SILVESTRI
Arranged by MICHAEL SWEENEY

00860014

From AN AMERICAN TAIL

SOMEWHERE OUT THERE

Words and Music by JAMES HORNER
BARRY MANN and CYNTHIA WEIL
Arranged by MICHAEL SWEENEY

OBOE
Solo

MCA music publishing

12

From **DANCES WITH WOLVES**
THE JOHN DUNBAR THEME

By JOHN BARRY
Arranged by MICHAEL SWEENEY

OBOE
Solo

From **DANCES WITH WOLVES**

THE JOHN DUNBAR THEME

By John Barry
Arranged by MICHAEL SWEENEY

OBOE
Band Arrangement

0860014

From The Paramount Motion Picture RAIDERS OF THE LOST ARK

RAIDERS MARCH

By JOHN WILLIAM
Arranged by MICHAEL SWEENE

OBOE
Solo

From The Paramount Motion Picture RAIDERS OF THE LOST ARK

RAIDERS MARCH

OBOE
Band Arrangement

By JOHN WILLIAMS
Arranged by MICHAEL SWEENEY

00860014

From APOLLO 13
APOLLO 13
(End Credits)

By JAMES HORNER
Arranged by MICHAEL SWEENEY

OBOE
Solo

MCA music publishing

APOLLO 13
(End Credits)

By JAMES HORNER
Arranged by MICHAEL SWEENEY

OBOE
Band Arrangement

0860014

MCA music publishing

From The Universal Picture E.T. (THE EXTRA-TERRESTRIAL)

THEME FROM E.T. (THE EXTRA-TERRESTRIAL)

OBOE
Solo

Music by JOHN WILLIAM
Arranged by MICHAEL SWEENE

MCA music publishing

THEME FROM E.T. (THE EXTRA-TERRESTRIAL)

OBOE
Band Arrangement

Music by JOHN WILLIAMS
Arranged by MICHAEL SWEENEY

Theme From The Paramount Picture STAR TREK

STAR TREK®-THE MOTION PICTURE

OBOE
Solo

Music by JERRY GOLDSMITH
Arranged by MICHAEL SWEENEY

STAR TREK® THE - MOTION PICTURE

Music by JERRY GOLDSMITH
Arranged by MICHAEL SWEENEY

OBOE
Band Arrangement

00860014

From The Universal Motion Picture BACK TO THE FUTURE

BACK TO THE FUTURE

OBOE
Solo

By ALAN SILVESTRI
Arranged by MICHAEL SWEENEY

00860014

MCA music publishing

BACK TO THE FUTURE

OBOE
Band Arrangement

By ALAN SILVESTRI
Arranged by MICHAEL SWEENEY

MCA music publishing